Financial Kingship

Principles to Unleash Kings In the Marketplace

Allan Rockhill

Financial Kingship
Published by Total Fusion Ministries Press
6475 Cherry Run Rd. Strasburg, OH 44680
www.totalfusionministriespress.org

ISBN-10:0988370077
ISBN-13:978-0-9883700-7-4

Scriptures are taken from the KING JAMES VERSION (KJV): KING JAMES VERSION, public domain.

Cover Design by Terry Ladrach
Cover Art by David Di Biase
Edited by Andrea Long

Library of Congress Control Number: 2013958039

Published in Association with Total Fusion Ministries, Strasburg, OH.
www.totalfusionminsitries.org

Dedication

This book is dedicated to those founding members of "Kings-net Ministries" who accepted the challenge of being my "guinea pigs" whilst God carved in us the principles that began our journey together. Thank you for believing what you could not see!

To Danny, Rod, Errol, Roy, Roland and Andre, may God continue to bless you as business kings in the kingdom and may he raise many more, in double portion anointing, around the world. May finance never be a problem to a local church's purpose!

Table of Contents

Preface

Over the years, God has brought various foundational scriptures to my understanding and I have gathered them together and fashioned them to shape the lives and mind-sets of His "business and market-related kings" that have been part of my ministry.

For the local church leaders to operate with "untied hands" there needs to be a review of God's economic policies, proving that they work even in the heart of a world-wide recession. This is one area in which the church will capture the modern world's attention. The church as a whole doesn't really lack anointed pastors, leaders, worship teams, children's church leaders, etc., but its impact on the world, in my opinion, is not where it should be. We don't chase money but we must understand its value in helping the church reach the lost. Too many churches don't progress sufficiently, the prime reason being that there just aren't sufficient finances to fulfill the vision they feel is from God. The end result of whatever we do in the church must focus on winning the lost and getting them established to be what God has designed for them. This lack of ready finance is one of the main causes for a weakened church front. In too many places around the world the church is still perceived as a poor neighbour on the block. Yet sitting in every God-ordained church are the people with the means to help establish the purpose of God where they are.

The foundational thoughts written in this book have helped many business and market-related kings come to terms with how God perceives them and what purposes He has for them. Many have drawn hope and inspiration from being associated, and it is my prayer that many more will as well.

Kings-net was founded on these teachings. I pray that God will use them to create in you the motivation to be the best "Business King" your potential suggests.

Introduction

We all need passion and drive to get us out of bed in the mornings, especially if your purpose happens to be conformed in one of the toughest arenas known to man.

As a Christian business owner or marketplace king, the last thing the devil wants is for you to succeed, particularly if you understand the call and purpose of God's destiny for you. If God has called you and anointed you to acquire wealth so you can be a conduit of blessing to your local church and the kingdom of God, when normal people go to work, it seems that 'kings' go to war. Market-related kings often encounter the most difficult hindrances and attacks, all designed to stop them prospering and gaining ground or to slow them down and frustrate them. Challenges are designed to intimidate them and cause them to slip into 'fear' mould, thus stifling the desire to succeed in the market place. Kings know what it's like to embrace the taste of warfare each day, and therefore they must have the passion and understanding of their purpose at the forefront of what they do and be able to come up with the motivation to press on when they need to.

Kings-in-business are designed to win battles and take ground and so warfare and finding solutions is part of their normal life. Now in the midst of these experiences, it's encouraging to realize that God has equipped you for success, that He has provided motivation for you to hold onto when tough places emerge, or to just know He has revelatory word to encourage you and strengthen your resolve for when you may need it. When Elijah thought he was done and dusted, God sent His angel to show that He cared.

May these key elements and revelatory principles in God's word help to equip you and sustain you in the winters of your endeavours. God will not be mocked. What He has called you to accomplish, is already a finished product, despite what may be evident in your 'Kingship' currently. The best motivation for you to begin each new day is the thought that, **"...for it is He that giveth thee power to get wealth..."** (Deut. 8:18). Therefore if God has called me to be a business king in the marketplace, then My Destiny is Wealth. Let's discover some of the motivations we can use to ensure that we reach our goals.

One

Prophet-Priest-King Revelation

"And Melchizedek king of Salem brought forth bread and wine: and he was the priest of the most high God. And he blessed him, and said, Blessed be Abram of the most high God, possessor of heaven and earth: And blessed be the most high God, which hath delivered thine enemies into thy hand. And he gave him tithes of all."

(Genesis 14:18-20)

This is one of the first and most powerful examples in the Word that teaches a principle of how finance and unlocked promises are released, so that the lack of money should never be a problem in any church's vision. The principal giftings are those of **Prophet-Priest-King** (in business) and they are shown to work here in synergy, with devastating effect. All though the Word, where this combination of Prophet-Priest-King was seen, it was a powerful time and demonstration of success. Samuel, David, and even Jesus all came in the manifestation of this dimension. So when you use this synergy in the realm of finance, your results will be amazing.

Prophets in their own right have the power to cause the heavens to open above and speak warning, direction, and confirmation to you.

Priests have the anointing to bless you and keep increasing your borders through pronouncing blessings over you. He is anointed by God to do this. **(Num. 6:22-27)**

Kings rule over areas and regions of land. In these regions, they exercise power, authority, and dominion. They are the final word in their domains. Everyone waits for the word of the king!

Abraham was a business king in our scripture reference. He was a solution provider and had an anointing to generate wealth. Yet he relied of the Prophetic word and the Priestly blessing to complete his financial kingship **(Gen. 14:18-19)**.

This is one of the first pictures we have of these three gifts operating together. Their synergy in the financial arena is noted. As Abraham gave a tithe of the spoil to his Priest (Melchizedek), the blessing that is prayed over him in return unlocked the promises of God to him **(Heb. 7:6)**. It was in line with the prophetic word preciously spoken over Abraham. God had delivered his enemies into his hand.

A financial strategy for God's business kings had been revealed as early as **Genesis 14**, in the book of first mentions. The direction, warning, or strategy of the Prophet, in conjunction to the unlocked blessing of the Priest, enables the business king to win and produce wealth (spoil) in the marketplace. It ends with the business king's generosity and his sowing into the kingdom. The business king has skill and anointing for the marketplace, but when in a synergy with the Prophet and Priest, his success is noted **(Gen. 14:14-23).**

Set men over congregations should learn the value of their purpose to their financial kings. They should grow financial sons in their houses by building a fatherly relationship with them, built on trust and the desire to grow them into their ministries, with success. They should provide accurate, prophetic input for them timeously so that they understand direction, timing, and strategy in their financial dealings. This, together with the blessing ministry of the Priests, is a significant force to power them to financial success. The set men's input and fathering towards these financial sons will culminate in them one day attaining what God had called them to do. With understanding, they become conduits of financial supply releasing provision so the lost can be won and the church can advance in its world mission. The church of Jesus is not the poor neighbour on the corner. It is the head and not the tail of God's influence in the world. For it to be unable to do what it needs to do in the world is just wrong. Having to raise funds to support itself or pay salaries suggests that God can't pay for what He has ordained. The world has seen in many places a wrong picture of God. He is not poor and He has no delight in poverty, especially since He provided the church with kings who are more than able to finance His mission. No church should struggle financially to get their Godly vision fulfilled. God has given the synergy of Prophet-Priest-King (in business) to the church. Those who discover its value benefit incredibly.

My Personal Motivation...

- I want to be the financial king God wants me to be.
- I will operate in the synergy of Prophet-Priest-King revelation.
- To understand as best I can this winning strategy that God has provided in the Word.
- Am I playing my part in how God wired me? Are my church and the kingdom of God advancing because I am participating to the best of my ability, in how I was anointed?

Two

My Destiny is Purposed Wealth

**"Beloved, I wish above all things
that thou mayest prosper and be in
health, even as thy soul prospereth."**
(3 John 2)

This prayer is an amazing motivation for all God's potential kings-in-business. There is a lot of negative religious pressure that can be quite daunting for the people who have been anointed to create wealth in the kingdom, and it can have a detrimental effect on those called to operate in the financial world.

John made it clear that **"above all things,"** a priority requirement must be that God's people and His financial kings are able to create wealth and have health in their bodies as well. The winning of the lost and the extension of the kingdom will always require financial outlay, and God's Kings are the prime candidates to handle this responsibility.

Therefore it is important for kings-in-business to accept that they are in the marketplace to create a wealth flow into the kingdom. Your destiny is that of being a conduit of financial wealth, pouring into God's people. You are primed to progress and impact the world of finance. You are anointed to succeed in its system. God's call on you is more than enough for what will oppose you. HE has designed that you prosper in this arena. You are supposed to succeed here. You are meant to make an impact in transferring the wealth of the world into the kingdom.

This is the purpose of the king-in-business and your generous giving will advance the purposes of God where you are, rapidly. God has taken **"the above all things"** seriously and wants to see you rise to the level of a wealthy, healthy, functioning financial king, that contributes to the stability and effectiveness of His church in the earth. Although seasons do change and tough economic times do occur, they actually should inspire rather than demoralize you. You are never on the world's economic plan. You are part of God's success strategy that He has established to succeed, no matter what the money markers indicate. You need to remind yourself of who called and purposed you into the marketplace and draw comfort from the Apostles of God who have dug this well in prayer already. It requires that we keep these financial wells open and not allow the Philistines to stop them up **(Gen. 26:18)**. Kings must grow their faith and expectations and be confident in the trust God has placed on their abilities. This well of prospering and being in health **"above all things"** was opened up for the church a long time ago and they should be aware of the tactics to close these wells permanently. The church needs finance to win the lost and advance the kingdom of God in the earth, and therefore a king's success in the marketplace is crucial to the plan of God. This is your arena. This is your mandate. Make it count.

All through the Word of God you will find examples of people succeeding and being able to turn from captivity, during times where the natural eye would only see the impossible. God has stated in His Word that, **"The things which are impossible with men are possible with God" (Luke 18:27).** Kings must introduce their impossible situations to the realm of the possible so that you create the platform to initiate change and channel success. God is never in a place that He does not know what to do with the difficulties that present themselves. He always has a plan to move forward, and if necessary, a replacement plan, so the original purpose is re-instated. You operate under the promise, **"...for it is he that giveth thee power to get wealth" (Deut. 8:18).** God is for you and therefore nothing can stand against you and prevail.

If you recognize that God has called you to be a financial king then you must accept that your kingdom destiny is wealth-creating. Don't struggle against religious mind-sets and the immaturity of unknowing people. Well-meaning people and their comments have before today, been the ruin of many with vision and purpose from God. Kings should not display arrogance but would do well to remember in these cases that it was God that called and appointed you. It was God who designed your Financial Kingship mantle to succeed in the marketplace. Not all well-meaning people in the church understand that making money and being prosperous can actually be a call from God. Therefore Kings must keep their focus on God and take direction from Him. Chasing money is not the plan. Fulfilling your call in creating a wealth flow is His plan. People who are not anointed in this dimension have a limited understanding of what financial kings are about and their comments can be quite off-putting. Remember they are at a different place in their walk with God and they didn't commission you. Your kingdom purpose is creating wealth and keeps the church as a frontrunner in the community. Why should what belongs to the name of our God be received as a sub-standard entity? The church and its purpose is not a joke. The Word it preaches has the power to bring people to Christ and salvation, and transform them into purpose for God. Kings play a crucial role in creating this platform.

As a financial king for God, you have been designed and chosen to be a conduit of blessing both in the local church and the kingdom. THIS IS YOUR CALL. This is the reason you were born. John the Baptist waited in the desert until the **"day of his shewing unto Israel" (Luke 1:80)**. This was his ordained purpose and the day eventually came when he was released to fulfill this plan of God. Being a king in business and creating a wealth flow is what you are about. You don't need to apologize for it, either. Being functional with wealth is what you are supposed to look like. This is natural for you. Providing spoil and increase for your visionary, is the fulfilled purpose of your kingship. Regardless of the economic season, you soldier on and work in your anointing to provide the resources from your tithes and givings so your set-man is able to fulfill the vision God has given him. You rejoice that your efforts will help establish this purpose and lead to the winning of the lost as well. Just as King David **"... brought forth the spoil of the city in great abundance" (2 Sam. 12:30)**, God has this expectation from your financial kingship as well. This is where you are fulfilled as a person.

My Personal Motivation...

- Is the relevance of my business as an anointing and call from God. It's important to God, so it must have great value to me.
- Is that God values me in this regard. He is trusting that I will respond with maturity and see His reasons for needing me to be successful.
- Is that my prosperity is a prayer that has gone up before God by anointed apostles in the past and I understand that this purpose is a desire in God's heart. It is not a carnal plan of man.
- Is that no matter how hard it becomes, my focus is on what God has asked me to fulfill and as I move toward it, it becomes achievable. Economic recessions and financial dry places will serve to prove that God's word works and the anointing to prosper in the marketplace will break the strangleholds of the enemy.
- Is the truth that **"...money answereth all things" (Eccles. 10:19)** and that it is not the anointing that is lacking, nor the worship or desire of God that really hinders a church's progress. Most can't get their vision moving along successfully, simply through a lack of finance. I am called to provide an answer to this problem. I am anointed to succeed in business for the greater purpose of reaching the lost for God and my giving enables the church to more efficiently reach those needing to be won.

Three

Spoil with My Name on It

**"...And he brought forth the spoil
of the city in great abundance."**
(2 Samuel 12:30)

Every business and marketplace king is in business to create wealth as God intended **(Deut. 8:18)** and make money for the kingdom and purposes of God in the local church as well as to provide adequately for their own needs. They go to "war" every day and gather in their "spoils" (profit) and gladly present their tithes and generous giving to the right spiritual authorities and oversight in their lives. Abraham returned with his spoils of war and gave Melchizadek a tenth of them all **(Gen. 14:20).** Abraham gave his portion to the **"man of God"** who was sent to him at that time. This led to so many breakthroughs in his life. One of the most significant breakthroughs according to **(Heb. 7:6)** was that Abraham, the one who had the promises, had them blessed or unlocked to operate for him. This is a huge benefit and blessing opportunity for all market-related kings who sow into the lives of their set-men.

This portion of scripture, apart from many other lessons, reveals the partnership that needs to exist between financial kings and their set-men. God has appointed Priests (set-men) and

Prophets to work with His business kings, and their gifting helps in causing the financial king to succeed in the market place. They in turn realize the part God played in their successes and find themselves in a position to be generous with their rewards. This capacity to give enables the church to advance rapidly in its quest to win the lost and be effective in its communities.

Business kings are anointed to "plunder" the marketplace and succeed in making large amounts of profit way in excess of what normal working people can manage. Kings in the biblical days had seasons when they went to war to plunder other kingdoms and gain revenue for themselves to help keep their own kingdoms afloat. **(2 Sam. 11:1)** David did this every year and the time he decided not to go, is the time when he got into trouble with Bathsheba. The more these kings gathered on these raids, the more their sphere of influence increased, which enabled them to balance the books and costs of their own empires. This is what kings did. They fought and gathered in the spoil. They increased their territories by subduing other kings in their area.

It's comforting to know that in my city and places of business trade worldwide, there is an abundance of "spoil" that has my name on it. My business has "spoil" available in these cities and it is set aside just for me. God has anointed me to prosper in business and ensured that I have the ability to plunder in each place, to affirm my business status and financial kingship. He knows exactly where it is to be accessed and even which people will provide it for me, or steer me towards its release. When Israel came to the Promised Land, God told them to go in and possess the **land** He had set aside for them. Each tribe and person had their own portion of inheritance. As a

19

business king for God, you have "land" that God has set aside for you. There may be a thousand other businesses just like yours, but God has still ordained **your** success in **your** land and that is where your spoil is waiting for you to discover and possess it. It won't go to anyone else. It belongs to you. You have to claim it and make it yours.

When Elijah needed to leave the Brook Cherith and move to another place of resource, God told him to go to Zarepath for He had instructed a widow to feed him and take care of him. The spoil that belongs to you has been arranged and set up by God so that you can benefit. It's amazing to realize that even the people who will contribute to your success, have been put in place to steer you towards your financial inheritance. Spend time praising God for His kindness and generosity. He has ordained a place of wealth for you. Your "land" has been earmarked for you. All you will ever need has already been put in place.

My Personal Motivation...

- When I leave for work today, I know that my city has "spoil" (profit, plunder) that has been set aside just for me. I am the only one able to claim it. It's in my name, just waiting for me to take ownership. I have "land" (a place, location) set aside for me from which I will prosper. God has actually designed it specifically for my business. Even if the competition is steep, it does not stifle what God has put in my "land" for me. Through righteousness, faith expectation, and consistent hard work, it won't be long before I start to accrue what God has set aside for me.

- Whatever I have missed out on in the past is still unclaimed. Only I can still retrieve it! Like Isaac of old, I will re-dig some of the wells that have not been as productive as they could have been, until I find "Rehoboth"—the one that will make room for me.

- God is not mocked, nor will He ever lead me astray. Since He has called me to be a business king for Him, then He has given me an abundance of "spoil" and it is waiting for me to discover it.

- I will make sure that what has been stolen from me in the past will be repaid in full. I am on a mission to find and claim what God has set aside for me in establishing me as a marketplace king.

- Today is the first day of the rest of my life. With renewed vigour, I will set out to be what God has ordained me to be. I will seek the advice of the men of God that have been placed in my life, as well as the counsel of financial mentors that God brings to me. I will study the principles that govern God's financial strategies and observe them diligently. I will do all I can to put myself into the place where I will collide with the "spoil" left purposefully for me. God needs me to succeed.

Four

Bundles Left Purposely in My Path

"And let fall also some of the handfuls of purpose for her, and leave them, that she may glean them, and rebuke her not."

(Ruth 2:16)

Ruth had decided to stay with her mother-in-law after they had experienced personal tragedy and hurt when they lived together in Moab. Her sister Orpah returned to Moab, never to be heard from again. But we still hear of Ruth. We are all presented with choices in life, but it is always wise to stay with the plan God has set as your purpose until that season is over. It was easy for Orpah to go back to what she knew rather than accept the opportunity that was being presented to her. Following the opportunities God presents will move you closer to your destiny and cause you to be in the position to collide with it.

Naomi returned to her home and told the people to call her *Marah* (bitter). She allowed her situation to control her and if it were not for Ruth, she would have struggled with the way she saw herself. Even though life may be challenging, God can still be 'God-to-you.' It's very important that you keep your hope and faith expectation where it needs to be. From the time these ladies returned, they had "to glean in another harvest field" for provision. For them to live, someone else had to be successful! Don't be put off by some of the experiences you may have had. You could be in training to collide with what God has in mind for you and one day, others will be kept alive because of your success. The amazing thing about the gleaning that Ruth was forced to do was the fact that the very fields she gleaned in as a struggling immigrant became hers a little later on, through her marriage to Boaz.

However, when it came to Ruth who was gleaning in Boaz's fields, he had already seen her and heard a great deal about the kindness and sacrifices she was affording a relative of his—Naomi. He told the reapers to do certain things for her that would be a blessing to her. Unbeknown to her, Boaz had arranged for her to bump into far more than she was expecting. Her expectation was a single stalk here and there, and to gather enough for her and Naomi to survive on. Boaz had arranged **"bundles of sheaves"** that were arranged and left purposefully in her path so she couldn't miss them. They were set there specifically and intentionally for her. Why wouldn't God do the same for His business kings today?

Go about your kingly business duties, as you need to do. God is watching your heart and continual acts of kindness and generosity. He has noticed the sacrifices you have made. Unbeknown to you, He has arranged financial deals, and good-sized ones, purposefully for you to bump into. You won't collide with them if you don't pursue your purpose, even through the mundane, daily routine of financial kingship. As you go about surviving from time to time, perhaps your prayer and faith should be an expectation, way beyond what you are gleaning at the moment. Remain thankful for the small deals that keep you alive but remain focused on the hope that God is setting you up to bump into measures of His kindness that are way beyond what is considered to be the norm. This is what He did for Ruth and God is not a respecter of persons, His Word says, **"Jesus Christ is the same yesterday, and today, and forever" (Heb. 13:8).**

My Personal Motivation...

- I understand that God is aware of where I am financially and what I have gone through in my business. I must trust that I am still in His best interests and even though it looks bleak, I must believe that HE is setting me up for better things.
- He has noticed my unselfish and sometimes sacrificial care of those around me and considered what I have given up so that others can benefit. He wrote that, **"The liberal soul shall be made fat: and he that watereth shall be watered also himself" (Prov. 11:25).**
- But it is my time now! He will lead me to the Boaz's of the business world and see to it that bundles of unexpected blessings find me in the paths of my purpose.
- Where I have felt like a stranger and a beggar, I sense that profile is about to change. I am about to be promoted from a survival mentality to one of ownership, where I provide for others.
- Even though in the present, things may look tough, I believe my future looks good and I will hold onto that. God sees what I don't. Hagar may have confessed in her most challenging times that she could not see a solution, but that didn't mean that God didn't have a plan to save her **(Gen. 16:13-14)**. Notice that the spring of water where the angel found her was between **Kadesh** and **Bered (v. 14)**. *Kadesh* means "a wilderness" and *Bered* translates to "hail and devastation." Even in the places of my wilderness experiences in business, and the times of economic devastation, God still sees what I don't. My future looks good, and I will hold on to that!

Five

Providing Grip and Balance

"But Adoni–Bezek fled; and they pursued after him, and caught him, and cut off his thumbs and his great toes. And Adoni–Bezek said, threescore and ten kings, having their thumbs and their great toes cut off, gathered their meat under my table: as I have done, so God hath requited me. And they brought him to Jerusalem, and there he died."

(Judges 1:6-7)

Adoni-Bezek was the ruling king over this particular area and this was where his sphere of influence and authority was the law. Those other "kings" (70 in number) and ruling princes that he had previously conquered were reduced to eating "scraps" from under his table because he had arranged, after their defeat, that their thumbs and big toes be removed. He reduced their physical ability significantly and left them dependant on his provision.

The removal of the thumb was symbolic of taking away the **strength** from a person's hand, and a big toe removed from the foot, signified that the **balance and stability** had been seriously reduced. Whenever a ruling king was captured and defeated by another, the strength and stability he previously displayed in his position of authority was symbolically removed, forcing these once powerful leaders to survive on "scraps" that would fall from their victor's table. A person with no thumb has very little grip in his hand, as the thumb is the key source of strength to the hand. Having a big toe removed plays havoc with your balance and sure-footedness and brings to the eye a person who looks wobbly and very unsteady. Victorious kings reduced their opposition to such physical specimens. They sent out the clear message that these captives, who once yielded great power and authority, were now worthless dependants, having lost the authority and power they once wielded.

Our enemy, the devil, has caused such religious confusion over finances in the church, that in many cases it has resulted in the church trying to live off of "scraps" in order to survive. God never designed the church to struggle to implement its vision or purpose in the earth.

When it comes to money in the church, it seems that so much insecurity and wrong understanding has been allowed to grow and develop. Television has helped to add to the confusion and uncertainties in people's minds. One group advocates this point whilst another has a different view altogether. Not many Pastors make a clear stance on what they really believe for fear of losing their congregations, and so the topic of finance has become a real source of division in the church. This division and confusion has successfully hampered the free release of wealth to the local church and has restricted its ability to impact on the community and its effect on ultimately winning the lost to Christ. A cash-strapped church is a sorry sight. In most cases it's not the anointing or the presence of God that is lacking. It is the evidence of "just enough" or "not enough" cash, so that the church struggles to become what God intended. Churches, who have the resources—that is, business kings—but have not turned them into financial sons and governors, are just like those captured kings with their thumbs and big toes removed. Satan has, and will continue to cause such confusion when it comes to money, that these kings who have the potential to be conduits of blessing, become confused and dejected about who or what they are supposed to be. Through this confusion and attack, our enemy has succeeded in cutting down the strength and stability a church should be displaying, and it is left in many cases, to be seen as the poor, struggling neighbour on the corner. Jesus taught that before you build a tower, you should make sure you have what it takes to complete it; otherwise you'll become the laughing stock of the town. I can't see God setting up His church on the earth to fail through lack of finances. God knew from the beginning that it would cost money to build the church and reach the lost.

So, each local church has within its members, the wherewithal to be financially viable. God has provided members to sow and tithe and be financial supporters of the purposes of God where they are. He has also placed in the ranks, business kings, those with an anointing to create wealth, to provide for the vision in unprecedented ways. These business kings have the ability to advance the purpose of the church at an unbelievable pace. They really form part of the "grip" and "balance" every local church requires. When this financial arm is out of order, the strength, stability and effectiveness of a church is seriously impeded. The church doesn't live off the scraps the devil affords it. The church is symbolic of God's power and authority in the earth, and finances form part of that front.

My Personal Motivation...

- I see my call in the kingdom as part of a function that creates a transfer of financial wealth.
- The more successful I become and the more generous I can be, actually helps in causing my local church to be strong and stable in our community.
- Generous and successful financial kings ensure the church moves away from a "living off scraps" mentality, to the category of a "Church on the move."
- I want to play my part and be a generous provider.
- I want to learn what it means to be a "financial son" in the house.
- I want to discover how to become a "financial governor" in the strategy of God. **(1 Kings 4:1-7)**
- In my financial kingship, I want to make sure that I form part of the team that gives my church it grip and balance in our community, so that the lost can be reached and redirected in God's plans.
- I am blessed to be in a position to be a conduit of financial giving. People will come to praise God more and more, and be touched in so many different ways, because the money our church needs to reach them is available.

Six

A Ram in the Bush

**"And Abraham lifted up his eyes,
and looked, and behold behind him
a ram caught in a thicket by his horns..."**

(Genesis 22: 13)

Abraham loved God so much and was obedient to him to the **'nth'** degree. However the greatest challenge came to him when God told him one day to offer, in sacrifice, his only son **(Gen. 22:2)** at a particular spot. This son was the "son of promise" that would begin his heritage on the earth. He would be the first in line to build a nation of people that belonged to God. Sacrificing him was a tall order and a huge challenge to his faith and trust in God especially after having to wait so long for him to be born. His other son, Ishmael, had not been God's choice for what He had in mind and Abraham had to release him and send him away with his mother. Now to be told to sacrifice Isaac on the altar was a real stretch for him.

He may not have understood the logic behind God's command, but he was able to believe that God was not a liar, and would raise the child from the dead if necessary, because of what He had already promised. **"He staggered not at the promise of**

God through unbelief; but was strong in faith, giving glory to God; And being fully persuaded that, what he had promised, he was able also to perform" (Rom. 4:20-21).

It goes on to say in **Hebrews 11:19** that Abraham, **"...Accounting that God was able to raise him up, even from the dead; from whence also he received him in a figure."** Through this obedient response, Abraham showed that he was prepared to do what God desired because he believed in God's integrity. Abraham unwaveringly understood that God would always fulfill what He has promised.

This is the message that all God's kings-in-business need to learn. God will not lie. What He has told you about your business will happen. He needs us to trust in HIS integrity. Despite what our circumstances are dictating to us and how real they are, and how devastating the outcome appears, God will always honour what He has said to you. This is the growth point for financial kings. Can I believe that I will not only get through where I am financially right now, but will I also be able to carry on being a blessing to the purpose of God? God's gifting on me to be a king-in-business will not change. God does not recall His gifting from us.

You as a business king for God may get to a stage where you are in great need. Recession has hit hard, and unless God comes through for you now, you fear you will be sunk. In the past you have used your business sacrificially to be a blessing to the purpose of God and obeyed the word on finance as best you could. You have tithed and blessed your man of God. You have given freely because you are a king-in-business. You have refreshed others when they needed it. It feels that this time, the season you have encountered is an extremely difficult one and there appears to be no way forward. This one is like a famine. It hangs on and on. You experience the same pressure day after day with very little respite. It seems that business has dried up and all resources have almost been depleted. This is when we need to draw comfort from the story of Abraham in out text. **God is just not able to fail those who have trusted in HIS integrity.**

Remember God has seen all you have done and understands what has been going on in your business. Your Kingship has definitely come up to God as **"a memorial" (Acts 10:4)** and He will make sure that in these times, you will discover supernatural provision. Abraham discovered a **"Ram in the Bush"** for his situation when God saw the obedience of his heart. When God saw how dedicated he was in trusting Him to the last detail of sacrificing his only son, Isaac, God knew that there was now nothing Abraham would ever withhold from Him. This really moved the heart of God and He said, **"And said, By myself have I sworn, saith the Lord, for because thou hast done this thing, and hast not withheld thy son, thine only son: That in blessing I will bless thee, and in multiplying I will multiply thy seed as the stars of the heaven, and as the sand which is upon the sea shore; and thy seed shall possess the gate of his enemies" (Gen. 22:16-17).** The "Ram in the Bush" was a supernatural supply from God on the hill of the Lord's provision. God's business and market-related kings have this same supply available. Abraham called the place, **"The-Lord-Will-Provide"** and it is said to this day, **"...In the mount of the Lord it shall be seen." (Gen. 22:14).**

Even in hurtful recessions and desperate times, God will not ignore those who have remained faithful to their call of generosity in providing finance for the kingdom. He has hidden nearby for you, provision of exactly what you will need, that you will suddenly discover at the right time. God has a miraculous supply of provision **"a ram in the bush"** ready for you to discover when it is most needed. Stay in expectation. Stay in living hope and faith. God sees what you cannot. He knows where the **"Ram"** is that will rescue you right on time. He will cause you to look up from where you are and see what has previously been hidden. Provision will suddenly appear. God did this for Abraham. There is nothing he will hold back from His business kings when He sees their sacrificial giving and generous hearts and the trustworthiness of His financial strategies. Look up. This could be the day you have needed for a long time.

My Personal Motivation...

- I will obey God in my business affairs, even to the point of giving sacrificially. He is God alone, and I serve gratefully the King of Kings.
- There will always be a **"Ram in the Bush"** provision for me. A miraculous deal that I may not see immediately. God has it hidden nearby. Like Ruth of old, it has been placed in my path for me to bump into when He knows it to be the right moment. **(Ruth 2:16)**
- I am confident and have faith expectation that God's supernatural provision will appear when I have need of it. I have remained faithful and so will He.
- I will learn to trust in God's integrity and not panic emotionally. I will remain quietly confident that what God has said will materialize when I need it to. He has a mount of provision where His resources lie in wait. His arm is not short in any way. He always has what I need.

Seven

The Seven Stages of Financial Blessing

**"Then Isaac sowed in that land, and received in the same year a hundredfold: and the Lord blessed him.
And the man waxed great, and went forward, and grew until he became very great: For he had possession of flocks, and possession of herds, and great store of servants: and the Philistines envied him."**

(Genesis 26:12-14)

**"And Abimelech said unto Isaac,
'Go from us; for thou art much mightier than we.'"**

(Genesis 26:16)

"...thou art now the blessed of the Lord."

(Genesis 26: 29)

Mankind places a measurement of success according to the training, achievements and experiences people encounter in life. Prosperity is relative: one man's bicycle is another man's car. Of the two, who is more successful? Going beyond what we know success to be places many of us on unfamiliar ground and it can lead to all sorts of religious and confusing thinking. People who are not used to accruing wealth often develop a sense of guilt when they do, as they have never before had to contend with such a measure of success. Should I own this much? Am I allowed to be this fortunate? Maybe a little less will be more acceptable and within the realms of "normal".

Our opinion of how much is allowed pales into insignificance when we see the stages of wealth that God set out in Isaac's life. Does God not say to us that His ways are not ours? Many of us struggle with the understanding of how generous God can be. Many don't achieve what God has ordained simply because they can't believe it is right to have what God shows as acceptable. Let's have a look at how God deals with Isaac and the stages of wealth that He has in mind for those who will venture out and trust Him for it. When Isaac obeyed God by staying where he was and sowing in the land where there was famine, he could never have imagined what was about to unfold. He believed God and sowed in the land even though it was naturally the wrong thing to do. This trusting behaviour and faith action has become of immense benefit to all of us today. Let's examine the results, in stages, in Isaac's life:

Stage 1: **Sowing before reaping.** You can't obtain a harvest without first sowing seed to get one. Isaac had been obedient to a specific request from God, and his obedience led to a hundred-fold return in the same year. This was God's starting point when He dealt with Isaac. Yes, it was an act of faith, on Isaac's part, because he had to believe he was hearing from God. The request came to him to stay in the place he was and plant in the height of a severe famine. To any farmer, this was a pending disaster. There was no sense in it. It was a completely unnatural request. No one will sow seed where there is no possibility of a return. Isaac believing He heard from God obeyed and reaped a hundred fold that same year. God's starting point with those who are prepared to believe what He says, is always rewarded. Isaac's starting point was a massive one hundred-fold return. If God is not a respecter of persons, why should His business kings expect anything less?

Stage 2   **"...And the Lord blessed him."** On top of the hundred-fold return, which would probably satisfy most business kings, God still added further blessing on him. The word "bless" has the following derivative meanings:

*To empower you to succeed

*To prosper you

*To pour out favour on you

*To benefit you

*To add value to you

*To make you like a gift

*To unlock exactly what suits you

After God "blessed" Isaac with the hundred fold return, He still found ways to benefit him, empower him to succeed and to show him His favour! As I have said, most business kings would be more than happy with the performance of a hundred-fold return, but God showed Isaac that it was just a starting point. There was still room for **"blessing"**. There is always much more than imagined with God.

Stage 3   **"...began to prosper..."** After the hundred-fold beginning stage and God's further blessing on him, this stage declares that in God's understanding, Isaac was now "beginning to prosper." He was now at a place where God was showing that Isaac who had come from nothing, was now beginning to be in the place of prosperity that God had in mind. So in God's mind, a business or market-related king is only starting to be prosperous when he has received the hundred-fold return and then is blessed to succeed even more!

Stage 4   **"...continued prospering..."** Whatever that previous stage resulted in, "when he began to prosper," God caused him to continue in more of the same. There wasn't a let-up or recession to slow things down. No deals fell unproductively to the ground. There wasn't a family feud or carnal fight from greedy relatives. God said that the previous stage of blessing continued with the same intensity. So it seems that when you get to the place of success you have desired to be in business, which you know would be the very best of what you could ever hope to achieve, and then you keep progressing further from that place, shows the increase God has in mind. We start to get to feel what God means when we read in the word that He is a **"much more God."**

Stage 5   **"...became very prosperous..."** I said earlier that prosperity was relative. One man's bicycle is another man's car. Our view and understanding of prosperity is limited to our experiences and backgrounds in life. We all have a level of what we feel is prosperous. I'm sure for most business kings, that level won't come close to God's view that we see at this stage.

38

When God declared that Isaac was blessed, and that he began to prosper and continued prospering until he reached a place of, "now you are very prosperous," I am not sure many would have even ventured to think that this is the place of success God had in mind. Most of us would have stopped at the hundred-fold return point. This is a stage where in God's book, you now have more than just money. Now you are a true "King" in finances, because your personal influence is taken seriously in your city and nation.

Stage 6   **"...the Philistines envied him."** When you talk about the Philistines, you are talking about a real thorn in Israel's side. They were the archenemy and the one nation that had no respect for them. Their attitude towards Israel was always that they were no more than servants. They were masters over Israel. **(Judg. 14:4 & 5:11 and 1 Sam. 4:8-9)**. So when Isaac had become so prosperous and carried a stature about him, the Word says that even the Philistines envied him. When the world gets jealous over Christians prospering as God intends them to, one phone call from such a business king has the ability to get even government officials to pay attention!

Stage 7   **"Mightier than we..."** At this stage, the world begins to recognize that you possess more than just money. You have become a real threat to their purpose. You are a real contender. Your wealth has turned into prominence, significance and stature. Abimelech, who was the king over the land where

Isaac's influence and stature had grown, realized that this foreigner, had become as influential, if not more so, than the stature he carried. In a nutshell, when the devil packs up to leave the area that you have influenced with your giving and kingship authority, and accepts you have dominion; then you have reached the place where all those ruling kings and worldly authorities come to make covenant with you or desire you to move on because they are rendered insignificant. Your stature and presence rules the land! They see they are defeated because, "...**thou art now the blessed of the Lord" (Gen. 26:29).**

This is the level God has in mind for His kings-in-business! Isaac got to this 7th stage of blessing because he dared to obey God's Word to him. God does not change. He is always the same. **(Mal. 3:6)** He has vision of your kingship success that is way beyond what you can think or imagine. Explore the possibilities. Don't stop short of the mark that God has designed for you. Your thoughts are not His. His degree of blessing is nowhere near where the natural mind will allow you to go. Always be alert to the voice of the Holy Spirit especially in difficult times, because obedience will always lead to you having the fat of the land in measures unimaginable.

My Personal Motivation...

- As God prospers me in business and in the marketplace, I will be sure to remove the religious blinkers from my eyes, so that I understand what HE actually means. He thinks outside of the box and does not conform to man's ways.
- I will need to operate above and beyond the religious tongues and carnal thoughts that will emerge. I will have to keep my mind on how God sees things and not what is dictated to me from others, and what they think are acceptable norms.
- It's clear from God's perspective that people's "acceptable norms" aren't the measuring stick either. I will have to become comfortable with supernatural abundance, and the various ruling figureheads who consider me a threat through the influence I now carry.
- I should aim to grow into these different stages of wealth that God has engineered for me and teach myself to become comfortable in them.

Eight

A Generous Spirit Will Protect You

**"But the liberal deviseth liberal things;
and by liberal things shall he stand."**

(Isaiah 32:8)

There are a number of significant truths we must understand from this verse, especially in the light of the uncertainties of our current economic situation. Markets are so unpredictable and can fall to record depths at any moment and take a long time to recover. People are nervous about investing and credit is hard to come by and so spending is not as it has been in the past. God knew all this was going to take place and so the word written so long ago is even more trustworthy for any sceptics out there. It's great to be able to read of God's solutions written thousands of years before you actually needed them. Having a spirit of generosity is vital in these times.

First, your generosity will result in you being able to withstand financial pressure no matter what the economic climate. This is not implying a "once–off" generous donation but rather a lifestyle of generosity. As a business king for God, I know that the market runs hot and cold. I just don't always know *when* it will suddenly fall or climb. However, this scripture assures me that I will stand in whatever economic season is prevalent because my business management has in its budget, a standard level of "generosity" to touch situations outside of its own needs. God promises that these acts of generosity will result in a company being able to stand resolutely and confidently amidst an unstable market environment.

Secondly, we must notice from this verse that "generosity" is a desired plan. Ways to be generous are worked out so that being generous is an assured end result. Budget meetings should include discussions on how and where to be generous. Our starting scripture reminds us, **"But the liberal deviseth liberal things..."** This needs to be part of the planning strategy to ensure financial returns when times are tough.

Thirdly, you must have the desire to be generous. From this desire to be generous, you will work out ways that this can be achieved and as you practice your heart of generosity, God promises that **you will stand**. That means even if other business practices with household names start falling through economic dips and uncertain markets, your promise from God is assured. You will still be standing and trading when the dust settles.

In summary, don't let the pressure of world events and market related business restrict you and confine you. You are on God's economic plan. Develop and maintain "a generous spirit." Find ways to be generous and watch how God works to keep you standing. You can't fail doing it God's way.

My Personal Motivation...

- As a business king for God, my call is to be a conduit of financial blessings into the kingdom and my local church. I won't be satisfied until I am accomplishing this.
- I must work hard, even in the tough times, to maintain a generous spirit. "Generosity" has fruit to it that will serve me well and preserve me always.
- I will look for ways to be generous. I will include in my budgeting ways to be generous so that my business always has a leading edge to it. People plan holidays for a specific time and season. I will plan to stand in the toughest economic times by devising ways to be generous.
- God loves a cheerful giver. I won't let the markets dictate to me because I accept that God has me on HIS economic plan. His plan works despite the natural outlook.

Nine

Exceeding Past Financial Records

"After these things the word of the Lord came unto Abram in a vision, saying, 'Fear not, Abram: I am thy shield, and thy exceeding great reward.'"
(Genesis 15:1)

Abraham had obviously put in place certain things that pleased and moved the heart of God. It says in this verse, that **"after these things,"** God's word came to him with a positive endorsement. Preceding this verse, and included in previous earlier chapters of Genesis, are all the dramatic and prophetic actions he was involved in, that bore witness with God. These involved his nephew Lot - his battle with Chedorlaomer - his historic meeting with Melchizedek and his decision to, **"...lift up mine hand unto the Lord..." (Gen. 14:22).**

In **Genesis 14** we see the valuable foundation laid down that ensured financial success:

- The value of sons in the house **(v14)**
- The role of Melchizedek in the role of prophet and priest **(v18,19)**
- The blessing of Melchizedek that released the promises of God over Abraham **(v20) (Heb. 7:6).**

- Abraham declaring that only God will make him rich **(v22-23)**

It was after these things had taken place that Abraham received news from the Lord that his faith actions had resulted in great benefit to him:

- There was no need to fear
- God would be his shield
- God would be his exceedingly great reward.

It is a wonderful place to be in life where you live in peace with the absence of fear. This is what it means when the word says, **"For he had dominion over all the region on this side the river, from Tiphsah even to Azzah, over all the kings on this side the river: and he had peace on all sides round about him" (I Kings 4:24)** and **"But they shall sit every man under his vine and under his fig tree; and none shall make them afraid: for the mouth of the Lord of hosts hath spoken it" (Micah 4:4)**. To be a business and market-related king in today's changing economy, the blessing of operating with the absence of fear is immeasurable. Now if you add to this the promise of God being your shield, you place yourself in a very good position to succeed in the marketplace. A shield in biblical days was mainly a defensive weapon. It could have been used as an offensive weapon, but was more useful in close combat, to protect the soldier from the potentially lethal blows of an opponent. It was lifted up to absorb the blows that were leveled with malicious intent against you.

It's comforting to note that God promised Abraham that **"after these things,"** He would be his **"shield."** He would see to his protection and safety in the heat of battle both offensively and defensively. He will throw your opponents off guard and absorb the harmful blows directed to defeat you. Added to this God also promises that He would be his **"exceeding great reward."** This word "exceedingly" or "exceeding" is also used in **Eph. 1:19** where Paul described, **"And what is the exceeding greatness of his power to us-ward who believe, according to the working of his mighty power"** In literal terms, the word "exceed" means to go past a previously recorded mark. An Olympic record is set when the athlete breaks a previously held record. In other words, he betters the record time of an event by creating a new record. This is also what God promised He would do for Abraham. One of the blessings God has in store for the business king is to exceed, or go past previous records and dealings He has already accomplished. As you work with God in the role of a business or market-related king, your expectation must produce the faith to believe that God will continue to exceed all His previous known dealings with you. You should move upwards and onwards at a steady pace, going from strength to strength.

However, the market-related king must take into consideration that Abraham set some things in place that were obviously important to God for Him to say what He did in **Gen. 15:1**:

(1) Abraham made sure that when Lot was separated from him, he was no longer unequally yoked. Lot was never part of God's end plan for Abraham, and so Abraham inadvertently picked up some baggage on the way. As soon as Abraham separated form Lot, suddenly the land from its length to its breadth became his. **(Gen. 13:6-18)**

(2) Abraham showed understanding of the value of "sons-in-the-house," a concept that God is using in these latter days to strengthen the Apostolic ministry worldwide. **(Gen. 14:14)**

(3) He allows Melchizadek to exercise the Prophetic and Priestly gifts over his business kingship, a strategy God has released to help business kings today with their financial breakthroughs. The synergy of the Prophetic and the Priestly gifts working together with the marketplace king is a revelation the church needs to use. **(Gen. 14:18-20)**

(4) Later we read in **Hebrews 7:6** that Melchizadek blessed the one who had the promises (Abraham). These promises were locked up in Abraham and then loosed when he was blessed by this man of God (Melchizadek). This is a vital strategy to understand when you are called to be a king-in-business.

(5) Then Abraham makes the declaration that no one except the Lord will get the honour of making him rich. He makes a stand early in his business kingship that he has lifted his hand to God and to God alone will he look for His provision. He sets about making sure that he will do things God's way when it came to money, because he was confident that God's ways worked. **(Gen. 14:22-23)**

"Now after these things…" God's heart is moved. The one thing a business king needs in his favour is the backing of God's heart when it is moved because you have acted wisely and maturely—when you have shown the quality of your "sonship" as a king-in-business. Focus on following God's financial strategies and watch Him cause you to "excel" in all areas of business.

My Personal Motivation...

God worked in the heart of Abraham to bring into place certain truths. Once the prophet-priest-business king roles were established, then God added more ability to excel.

- As I allow the role of prophet- priest- king to operate as a covering for me in business, God causes me to come to the place where I operate without fear, where He is a shield and an exceedingly great reward.
- I must make sure I operate as a "son" in business. Sonship is a strength the enemy cannot deal with.
- I know I have promises that are not yet functional in my life, but I now know the way God will see them loosed for my benefit. I won't hold back on blessing my man of God financially so he can release blessing on me and be a catalyst to unlock the promises over me.
- If I am going to follow God's way to handle finance, then I must do it seriously. I must commit to what the word teaches and not put my slant on it or obey only when I feel that I can. Abraham was committed to making sure that God would make him wealthy and he determined to follow God's plan, from then onwards, to become financial stable and wealthy according to God's methods.
- As a business king I must accept that God's financial strategies and methodologies have always worked, no matter what the economic climate and therefore I will accept and follow them without hesitation.

Ten

The Value and Pursuit of Wisdom

"I love them that love me; and those that seek me early shall find me. Riches and honour are with me; yea, durable riches and righteousness. My fruit is better than gold, yea, than fine gold; and my revenue than choice silver. I lead in the way of righteousness, in the midst of the paths of judgment: That I may cause those that love me to inherit substance; and I will fill their treasures."

(Proverbs 8:17-21)

Proverbs 8 is talking about the value and role that "wisdom" has to offer in the way things are done. From **(v22-30)**, the word shows us the importance that wisdom was to God, even when He created and established things. It says of wisdom, **"Then I was by him, as one brought up with him: and I was daily his delight..."** **(v30)**, so wisdom was beside God when he designed and initiated all things.

Business kings must understand that though they may have a skill for business and market-related things, perhaps even an anointing, **"get wisdom"** is still essential in their make-up and success plans. It is the master craftsman in all their activities. Solomon was probably the wealthiest of all the kings of Israel, and yet he hardly spoke about finances. He did, however ask God for wisdom to be able to rule his people and spoke at length about it as well. The other side of achieving, gaining, and accruing financial wealth through giving and the practice of the financial principles in the word, is the gaining of wisdom. Whatever we do we are exhorted to "...get wisdom..." (Prov. 4:5-7).

Finding out the proper application of how the word works requires a diligent search and a gaining of wisdom if you are to know the secret things of God. I read somewhere, and agree that knowledge gathers facts and information and that understanding takes place when these facts are ordered correctly. Wisdom results when you apply this knowledge and understanding correctly. As a young Christian many years ago, I became quite frustrated reading Proverbs because of the need to understand and have wisdom. I didn't know what wisdom was, but the book of Proverbs kept telling me to get it. I prayed earnestly for an answer and one day the Holy Spirit answered me saying, "Wisdom is the proper application of the knowledge of God." A business king has an obligation to study the word and search out its truths particularly those that pertain to financial matters. Wisdom is an acquired thing. It's not automatic.

A great part of the business king's portfolio is to gain wisdom, because it will lead to financial blessing.

- **"I love them that love me... riches and honour are with me" (Prov. 8:17-18)**

- **"...That I may cause those that love me to inherit substance; and I will fill their treasuries" (Prov. 8:21)**

- "Happy is the man that findeth wisdom... length of days is in her right hand; and in her left hand riches and honour..." (Prov. 3:13-16)

There are no short cuts to getting wisdom. It must be a pursuit of any business or market-related king. Wisdom is the master craftsman in all your endeavours, and leads to wealth as a fruit.

My Personal Motivation...

- Being a business king for God is an absolute honour and privilege.
- It's not all about raw skill, luck, and inheritance; nor does it only know about the value of giving and the power of seed.
- The greatest asset to me gaining the wealth God has in mind is established in the pursuit of wisdom. Finding out how God's word is applied correctly will lead to the wealth that comes through finding wisdom.

Eleven

The Power of Seed

"Now he that ministereth seed to the sower both minister bread for your food, and multiply your seed sown, and increase the fruits of your righteousness."

(2 Corinthians 9:10)

The other side of "wisdom" as we looked at in the previous chapter, is for the business kings to realise the **"power of seed"** when it comes to cash flow requirements and having sufficient finances to do what God needs them to do. As long as you plant "seeds" in good ground, there will always be a return.

God makes sure that the business king—or anyone for that matter—who sows "seed", will always be supplied seed to sow and be in a position to reap a financial harvest. Therefore, those who sow seed will increase their capacity to sow, and always be in a position to gather in an increasing harvest. God's economic plan works, in one way, on the basis of what you sow is the same measure of what is returned. The secret is to separate your seed from your bread. Once you have that right, you are on a course to see harvest after harvest manifest in your life.

All through the word you will find reference and encouragement "to sow seed" or be a giver because of the power

54

you release and the promise of return when you do. In the business world, one of the tools that are employed to sell products and enlist new clients is the tool of marketing. You are invited to participate because of the good returns that will occur for your business, and from the client's perspective, your product becomes very appealing. You are encouraged and motivated to buy because the deal is just too good to pass up. God's word also motivates us to be sowers of seed and generous givers, and if you read past the ink, you will notice that the word of God motivates us through the promise of great returns.

- **But the liberal deviseth liberal things; and by liberal things shall he stand."**

  (Isa. 32:8)

- **"The liberal soul shall be made fat: and he that watereth shall be watered also himself."**

  (Prov. 11:25)

- **"Honour the Lord with thy substance, and with the firstfruits of all thine increase: So shall thy barns be filled with plenty, and thy presses shall burst out with new wine."**

  (Prov. 3:9-10)

- **Then Peter said, 'Lo, we have left all, and followed thee.' And he said unto them, 'Verily I say unto you, There is no man that hath left house, or parents, or brethren, or wife, or children, for the kingdom of God's sake, Who shall not receive manifold more in**

this present time, and in the world to come life everlasting.'"

(Luke 18:28-30)

I do not wish to make your service or financial kingship feel inappropriate or cheap in any way, but the word of God does encourage us to "sow" with a promise of assured return. Pastor Mike Murdock has an entire chapter on this concept in his book, *"31 Reasons People Don't Receive Their Financial Harvest"*. He shows clearly that God motivated through a promise of supply.

You cannot be a really successful business king for God and not practice and believe in "the power of your seed" that is in your hand and needing to find good soil for planting. Your seed in God's hand has the potential to return a supernatural harvest for you to utilize for God. Explore the hidden power of a seed sown into the good soil in the kingdom. God cannot lie, nor will He tell you something He didn't mean. The more you discover the value of what your seed can return to you, the more your capacity grows to be a financial king in the Kingdom. The results of trusting the principles of God's financial system will become self-motivatory and a sheer delight. As business kings, we will best serve our financial call when we grow from being entrepreneurs in the marketplace, to governors who know no lack. **(1 Kings 4:27)**

Why would God encourage His people through a promise of supply if the word were not true? God even tells us in Malachi to test Him in this concept of tithes and offerings. Here we see firsthand a challenge from God to trust what He says with a motivation that promises a return of supply. Money answers all things **(Eccles. 10:19)**, and so being able to grow your asset value and cash flow situation, is perfectly acceptable in God's plans for you. Jesus knew the value of money and spoke hundreds of times on the subject. Invest in the Kingdom of God and you will get the returns that God promises. Investing in God's financial system is the safest and surest way to prospering in life.

My Personal Motivation...

- God has just underlined for me a promise of definite, abundant returns, where I will have "bread" to eat and "seed" to sow that will keep the miracle of provision reoccurring.
- God motivates His business kings to be faithful givers with the promise of full barns and overflowing vats. I'm in! I want to fulfill my purpose in the kingdom. This is a way to be a successful participator.
- Religious thinking will not allow me to see the promise of supply for my endeavours in sowing seed. God knows the importance of finance in the 21st century and shows us ways to be able to access it. Money is useful and vital. It's the love of it that is dangerous. I will not turn away from the principle that God motivates business kings through a promise of healthy returns. Instead I will study and understand them, so that I can increase my stature of "Financial Kingship."

Twelve

The Power of Your First Fruit

**"For if the firstfruit be holy, the lump is also holy:
and if the root be holy, so are the branches."**

(Romans 11:16)

The implication of this verse reveals for us the importance of our attitude towards the "first fruit" offering. This first fruit offering is holy to God, and if it is done correctly, it ensures that the rest of the lump will be holy as well. In other words, the blessing that is released on the first fruit will filter through the whole batch, so that the same level of blessing will permeate through all aspects of the batch.

Prov. 3:9 instructs us to, **"Honour the Lord with thy substance, and with the firstfruits of all thine increase,"** and as we do so, the rest will be blessed so that our barns will be full and our vats overflowing. God's blessing will go past the first fruit and be also on all that remains. If you think about it clearly, God has just endorsed that your tithe as a first fruit of your giving will stretch to the remainder of your cheque as well. If we fall into the trap of thinking about how we will manage on nine tenths of our salary only, this promise of God tells us not to worry. God will see to it that the rest is holy to Him as well. He will ensure it will be sufficient to deal with what has to be done.

The first fruit offering is seen originally in **Gen. 4:4-7.** In the book of first beginnings, God reveals the value of first fruits. Abel gave the **first** of his flock and their **fat** to the Lord. He didn't wait to see if there would be a second. He gave to God the best of his flock, the firstborn, which is the sign of his strength. This is what God's Business Kings need to address. When it is time for dividends, the fruit of all your labour, it is time to give God His "First Fruit". Give Him first, from the fat and strength of your labour and He will bless the whole batch. Cain did not. God chose Abel's sacrifice. Your offering will be a "choice" one also, if it is the best of your returns. Give to God the first of your fat. Show God how you view Him and what emphasis you place on Him. Don't give him a smattering of what's left at the end of the line. Make sure that you give your "first" to the one who is the "first."

Giving to God first will lead to the process of filling your barns and causing your vats to overflow! When the barns are full you have both seed and bread. One sustains you physically; the other is sown to ensure you always have seed to sow and you can guarantee returns. When vats are overflowing, you have excess. You can pay your bills and still have leftover money, which grows into a nice cash flow situation for your business.

My Personal Motivation…

- The first fruit of my salary and first fruit of my increase in each business transaction will be given to God. No more excuses. I know how important the advice of my accountant is, but God's advice is above that. I know how my money can be lost in the system once it goes into the account, so I will devise a way that God gets His first.
- I have a job to do. In order to be a conduit of blessing and one who can advance the kingdom rapidly, I need to have the returns God wants me to have. I will follow His processes—my first to Him who is "the first"
- I don't just want to say that I am on God's economic plan and not on the worlds—I want to experience it firsthand. Therefore it is time to renew my mind and allow a different spirit to take precedence in my financial kingship, if it's not there already.
- The sooner I make these changes, the sooner I position myself to become what God has designed for me.

Thirteen

Anointed to Create Wealth

"But thou shalt remember the Lord thy God: for it is he that giveth thee power to get wealth, that he may establish his covenant which he sware unto thy fathers, as it is this day."

(Deuteronomy 8:18)

God swore a covenant oath of blessing in Abraham's life **(Gen. 22:16-18).** The seed of Abraham also fell into this category. Those who will work with God and observe to uphold the ways of God will live and multiply and gain possession of the land (all that God would have for you), as He swore to our fathers **(Deut. 8:1).** The promise is out there for us to walk in and claim through understanding and application of the principles of God.

The creating of wealth through the power (capability) that God has given His business and market-related kings is not in question. God tells us that it is He who has given us power to create wealth and we must see that wealth is CREATED. God expects you to have the fruit of wealth because it was a covenantal promise to Abraham. What God is concerned about is how you will behave when you obtain the wealth He has in mind for you. Will you still remember Him as your God and the One who has blessed you to have this level of created wealth? Will you remember why you have been given this measure of wealth? This is part of a business king's battle.

Looking at **Deut. 8:7-17**, we can see that God brings us to a place that He declares and considers to be a **good** land. It's a land that has a flow of water to keep you alive. It's a productive land filled with opportunities to prosper and bring in blessings. It's a place where He says because of it, you will lack nothing **(Deut. 8:9)**. You will eat well and live in beautiful homes and life will be good. He has empowered this measure of success for you. This is your potential. But when all this is operating in your life, will God's goodness and created wealth cause you to be complacent and forget all about Him? The danger of wealth (if your heart is not set on God), is that you will begin to think and feel more highly of yourself than you ought to **(Deut. 8:17)**. You will start to feel that you are responsible for the flow of wealth you are experiencing.

God is not worried that you can become wealthy. He has promised blessing in His covenant to Abraham and his seed. You should be moving down that path. But how valuable is God and His purpose to your life when wealth is such a great part of it? This is the challenge that will determine your true financial kingship! Do I still honour God as I should, or do I find excuses for the money I now have? The promise of created wealth is not an issue from God's perspective. In **Deut. 8** He underlines the fruit of the potential in your land:

    1)   **"A land of wheat, and barley, and vines, and fig trees, and pomegranates; a land of oil olive, and honey" (v8)**

63

2) "A land wherein thou shalt eat bread without scarceness, thou shalt not lack any thing in it…" (v9)

3) "Lest when thou hast eaten and art full, and hast built goodly houses, and dwelt therein;" (v12)

3) "And when thy herds and thy flocks multiply, and thy silver and thy gold is multiplied, and all that thou hast is multiplied ;"(v13)

There is no shortage to the way God intends you to be blessed. The only concern He has is that when you are, you will forget Him **(v11, 14, and 17)**. This is why your heart must be set on God—because of the danger that lurks when money is in abundance. A true king-in-business has overcome this battle.

My Personal Motivation...

- My expectations about whether I should become wealthy have changed for the good. God has just confirmed that He has given the power to His kings to do just that. I have ability from God to create wealth.
- I have the capacity to get the wealth that I am destined for. It is no longer a dream or possibility. It must become an expectation in me.
- Remaining humble, in love with God, and seeing Him as my only resource, is a challenge to those who have abundant wealth! So I will make sure that I honour God with my possessions and with the first fruit of all my increase. There is no limit to the wealth God has in mind for me. God's idea of wealth is way beyond what I imagine.
- I will not fall into the trap of thinking I am responsible for my creative wealth. I will keep my focus on the one who is the first. After all it is He who has called me into this kingship. I have a choice to obey His expectations as a financial provider, and I want to please Him.

Fourteen

The Recovery Plan

"And Adam knew his wife again; and she bare a son, and called his name Seth: For God, said she, hath appointed me another seed instead of Abel, whom Cain slew."

(Genesis 4:25)

The spirit of ungodly people in the marketplace is generally one of greed and success by any means possible. **Jude 11** talks about **"the way of Cain,"** and he is one of the characters in this scripture. Cain killed Abel because he was jealous of God's acceptance and preference of Abel's personal "offering." Marketplace people, who have gone "the way of Cain" are only out to succeed for themselves and will be highly agitated if others seem to be making it before them. They appear to have no fear in getting what they want by whatever means. Greed can manifest in ruthless ways.

There have been many deals and opportunities that have suddenly been stolen away from God's financial kings. They have needed those deals desperately and this action has left them reeling and gasping for life in the marketplace. If not careful, God's financial kings can seek revenge and go on a mission to do likewise, reducing themselves to the carnal levels of these competitors. Before you rush off in anger, stop to think for a moment about how God brought **"Seth"** into Adam and Eve's lives when they were robbed of their heritage. God provided for them and will do so for you.

Eve was so named because her name meant, **"...The mother of all living" (Gen. 3:20)**. She was the chosen vessel through which mankind would find life. It was to begin in her, and as a woman, she was fulfilled in her purpose when Cain and Abel were born. However, that dream was shattered in a single moment of a day. She woke up one morning with her life intact and her purpose being fulfilled. She was a picture of content. But by the end of that day, she was a mess. Her life had been completely overturned. Her purpose from God had been stolen from her. Her destiny as the one, who gave life in the beginning, now lay in a crumpled mess on the floor at her feet. Cain killing Abel created all this for her.

Such tragic circumstances, yet they are not uncommon to man. When all seems finished and there is nowhere to go, God has a recovery plan for you and your purpose. As far as Eve was concerned, He had "a replacement" in mind, one that would restore the original promise and purpose. When she became pregnant again, God gave her Seth, which means **"a replacement"** for what she had been promised previously. All of Eve's hope and purpose was suddenly returned and her life gained momentum once again.

This principle is the same for God's financial kings when they lose what they consider to be a crucial deal or opportunity for them. It might be the one deal above all others that have the capacity to take you to another level, only to discover that it crashes to oblivion. All joy and hope of going on seems to desert you.

You feel as helpless as a fish flapping aimlessly on the ground—but God has a **Recovery Plan** for you. When people steal away the opportunity you had to suddenly collide with your financial destiny, try to remember Eve's story and God's remarkable recovery plan for her situation. God always has a replacement deal to compensate you for what was taken. He is never caught without an answer for you. He sees and knows all things. Even though Eve was named as she was, God knew that her destiny would be challenged suddenly one day, but already had the "replacement" plan in place for the right time in her future. Therefore it would be good practice for God's business kings to declare the following with expectant faith when things of this nature appear:

"Even though I may feel robbed of my opportunity
to strike something big in my business status for God,
God is with me. In no time, this loss will be recovered by
God's replacement deal, seven times greater than what was
stolen from me".

My Personal Motivation...

- God is in control. He knows the beginning from the end.
- He has an amazing recovery plan. He always has a replacement deal in the wings. It is backed by His word, that if something is stolen from us, it must be replaced seven times more.
- I will work hard to produce what God has set aside for my business, and will always feel secure knowing that He has recovery in His thinking. It is not only recovery, but a full replacement of His original plan.

Fifteen

Season of Gain

"And it came to pass, after the year was expired, at
the time when kings go forth to battle, that David
sent Joab, and his servants with him, and all Israel;
and they destroyed the children of Ammon, and
besieged Rabbah. But David tarried still at
Jerusalem."

(2 Samuel 11:1)

There are a number of key elements that need looked at
in this scripture, but I want to concentrate mainly on the timing
and the different seasons of business gain.

Notice that it was **"...after the year was expired..."**—
which we might call springtime—that kings went out to war.
This was the time of "ingathering"—the time that made it
possible for armies to move (after long cold winters) and the
time for them to gather as much spoils as possible. Attaining
these target margins increased the ability to govern their own
lands adequately. They needed income in their treasuries to
balance their budgets, and so there was a time when kings went
to war. Notice also that nations, regions, and cities weren't to be
complacent in the off-season, either. If you didn't fortify what
you had and re-look at your defense systems to see how to
improve them or increase them, you became a target of other

70

kings set on plundering you! So part of the strategy to remain a strong nation was the in-house inspection of what you had, as well as the strategies to plunder others so that your treasury was financially sound. So there was a specific time when Kings went to war.

We must also realize when most ordinary people go to work every day, business and financial kings actually go to war! They go to a battlefield. Their work is carried out in the toughest known arena of the world—the business and marketplace—where ethics and niceties no longer abide. If the enemies can cut you out of a deal or create the opportunity to get it for themselves, they will! You have to go hard and focused at your targets in the marketplace. You have to be skilled and primed if you are going to succeed. Perhaps a better description would be a battle-hardened, seasoned champion.

What the business and financial kings need to realize is that there are times you do well and even really well, and times when you don't. In the off times, that's the time to re-look at your business or marketplace strategies and determine if they are still current and cutting edge. Are they still capturing the interest of the public eye and attracting investors from elsewhere? It's also a time to heal and re-establish ground that may have been lost in the heat of war. During this time, you must prepare yourself for the next season, not only your defensive strategies, but also your offensive ones!

Pray, intercede, clarify with God your targets, budgets, and profit margins. Bring them before God with faith and expectation, and plan your success so that you climb the ladder of influence and significance. God has made you a king in business. You need to succeed and produce a great profit margin. You are a conduit of blessing to your local church and the kingdom of God. The more you have to give, the quicker the kingdom will advance. So in the times and season of plunder; do well. Do extremely well and maintain your generosity. Stay focused on your given purpose.

Your opportunities to succeed may also become challenged by our enemy. For some reason, David chose not to do what kings did in the springtime, and he soon discovered a major distraction as close as the next house, that cost him dearly later on. The enemy is always looking for ways to plot your downfall and we need to be sharp and smart. As my business success increases, so do the distractions. Although Joab did a good job for David, he wasn't positioned to spearhead David's call and anointing. Remember that the distractions are levelled at getting you out of your place of effectiveness as a business king for God!

My Personal Motivation...

- Success can also be seasonal. I need to use and manage the season of plunder effectively.
- I should aim to become proactive even in the quieter times. Prepare my "defence" and strengthen "offensive" tactics. Quieter business periods don't mean that there is nothing to do. It's a time to re-look at how I do things and discover how effective I am. It may be time to initiate changes to make things more proactive.
- I need to be on the lookout for the distractions and curve balls the enemy wants to throw at me so that I am fully prepared to progress.

Sixteen

The Thousand-Fold Blessing

"The Lord your God hath multiplied you, and behold, ye are this day as the stars of heaven for multitude. (The Lord God of your fathers make you a thousand times so many more as ye are, and bless you, as he hath promised you!)"

(Deuteronomy 1:10-11)

Jesus taught in the parable of the sower that seed falling on good ground could yield as much as a thirty, sixty, or even one hundred-fold return **(Matt. 13:8)**. The different soil conditions of the heart also play a major role in the return your seed could create. Business kings should keep in mind that their prospering is much of a heart attitude as it is a turnover of numbers.

Most business people would be happy with thirty, sixty, or one hundred-fold returns for their endeavours. After the deductions and miscellaneous costs that appear out of nowhere, to get as high as a 30% return is more than acceptable and welcomed by many. However, good ground can and does produce higher yields. As God's business kings, we should have the expectation that our yields will always exceed the 30% mark.

But, when I see the **blessing** that Moses prayed and pronounced over Israel in **Deut. 1:10-11**, I know that business kings should lift their games. They should aim higher with their expectations. Even though Israel had increased from just Jacob's family arriving in Egypt, around 75 people, to the millions that stood with Moses at that time, Moses still released a blessing of a one thousand-fold increase over them as a nation. He blessed them with the future in mind, and that is what financial kings should be looking at as well. It's not just about now and having "enough." What about the future and the principle in Genesis of **a seed within a seed**? Everything that God made in creation for us, has seed within itself to reproduce again. This is how business kings should approach their level of growth in prayer. What have I got here that will keep producing new seed and new ground for me? The thousand-fold mark of blessing is the level you should aim at because it has heritage attached to it.

Moses understood that God was capable of much more than what normally meets the eye. **"With God all things are possible" (Matt. 19:26).** Unless you tap into what God has for you, you won't receive what is possible. Priests or set men and women over congregations should be teaching their business kings that higher returns are not out of their reaches. God has no problem with His business kings prospering way above the norm. Religion will teach us that when we have increased, then that is enough. But when is "enough" with God? He is prepared to go to the thousand-fold return mark.

Think about that thousand-fold blessing over your business. Think about the effectiveness that it would create through the opportunities that would appear. Think about the ability it would produce to give freely into the kingdom, large amounts of finance that could advance the purpose of God on the earth at a rapid pace. The world increases in areas of technology and discovery at an alarming rate and so our world changes all the time. So must the church. You can't really affect or impact for God in an advancing world with archaic ideas that we deem acceptable. A cutting edge church is a standard that is the norm in the world. People live like this every day trying to carve out a level and standard of living for themselves, so why shouldn't the church forge forward in keeping with the changing world. Business kings should not be afraid to aim higher than others do. This thousand-fold mark is a blessing the business kings should be familiar with.

My Personal Motivation...

- The levels of profitable returns for business are acceptable in the thirty-fold margins. Anything above this mark is considered amazing.
- From what I now understand, it is possible to believe that God is able to produce returns of one thousand-fold. This is the area that Financial Governors will operate in. Moses released the blessing for Israel to do so, even though they were already a great number. Moses was also considering the future of Israel as a nation, and not just their immediate needs.
- I will not stop at significant increases in my turn over. I may be falling short of what God wants to release to me. I will learn how to speak blessing and live with the expectation that my business under God knows no bounds!
- I can be much more of a financial king than what I am seeing at the moment.

Seventeen

A Purpose Fulfilled

"Now in the first year of Cyrus king of Persia, that the word of the Lord by the mouth of Jeremiah might be fulfilled, the Lord stirred up the spirit of Cyrus king of Persia, that he made a proclamation throughout all his kingdom, and put it also in writing, saying, 'Thus saith Cyrus king of Persia, The Lord God of heaven hath given me all the kingdoms of the earth; and he hath charged me to build him an house at Jerusalem, which is in Judah.'"

(Ezra 1:1-2)

The happiest and most content place any person or ministry in God can attain is the place of **your day of manifestation.** John the Baptist waited in the desert, waxing strong in the spirit, until the day of his manifestation **(Luke 1:80).** Discovering what you were born to do, is a realization and understanding that is hard to explain in words. Suddenly you step into the dimension for which you were made. It is a totally new experience. You realize the reason for your life. Your purpose becomes so clear and you become a person who is focused on the meaning of your own existence. Even though things in life may appear hard, you don't seem to struggle any more. You know what you are about and what it is that God has ordained for you to be and do. You're in your sweet spot—the place of your anointing. You have suddenly collided with exactly what God had in mind for you and the reason you were born. You are all God has wanted from you! Your striving has ceased. Even though tough times emerge, they don't necessarily slow you down because you have discovered your purpose and why you were created. The plan God has for you, has become the drive and motivation within you.

The prophetic word of Jeremiah stirred a release in Cyrus, king of Persia, to do and be what God intended from him. God's Word has power to cause you to live and focus and discover destiny. Cyrus understood that he was to provide the finance and resources to **build a house** for God in Jerusalem. As king, his resources were abundant and he had the ability to carry out this mandate from God. He began to see the reason for his position in life. God had chosen him to finance the project He had at hand.

This is also the mandate of God's financial kings. They are purposed to **build God a house** on the earth. They are anointed to create wealth and cause a flow of finance and resources to be released so God's purposes on the earth can be established. Just like Cyrus, they are chosen vessels and are given specific ability to create wealth for the kingdom and the local church. Their giving builds the purpose of God on the earth and in the communities in which they operate. Cyrus discovered God's plan for him through a prophetic word of Jeremiah, **"...the Lord stirred up the spirit of Cyrus king of Persia, that he made a proclamation..." (Ezra 1:1)**. God must speak to the heart of His business kings. One way He does that is through the prophetic word. Cyrus was stirred up in this manner and it led him to do something. If you look at the book of Haggai you will see again how the word from the Prophet stirred a reaction in the people until a solution was found for their financial indiscretions. Let the **prophetic** stir your heart and the **blessing** of your set man (or priest) shape your purpose, so that you move ever closer to **the day of your manifestation.** There is nothing more gratifying than to be in the place of your calling—the place to which you were assigned before you were born. Discovering that place is truly the fulfillment of your Godly purpose.

When does a financial king reveal he has reached the day of his manifestation? I believe it is when he has reached his sweet spot as a financial producer and giving generously is no longer a struggle for him. He has transitioned from planning and wanting to give, to being a generous giver, where he sees the kingdom advancing rapidly. That's what he was born to be!

My Personal Motivation...

- To get to the place where I am in my zone—the sweet spot of my purpose. I want to operate naturally as a conduit of financial blessing.
- To be the business king and provider that God has designed for me to be in the kingdom.
- To place myself under a prophetic anointing and the counsel of financial mentors, so that I hear the voice and mind of God as He speaks to me, causing me to become inspired to think ahead in terms of heritage and increase, which He has promised way beyond the norm.
- With God all things are possible. If He can stir the heart of a King outside of the covenant of God and use him as an example of how to be business king for God, then I have my purpose drawn up for me.
- I am anointed to contribute to the establishing of God's purpose on the earth. Therefore my destiny is wealth. I'm going to go all out to be a conduit of blessing in the kingdom.

Eighteen

The Hidden Treasure

"And I will give thee the treasures of darkness, and hidden riches of secret places, that thou mayest know that I, the Lord, which call thee by thy name, am the God of Israel."

(Isaiah 45:3)

Cyrus, a king of Persia who was outside of the covenant of Israel, was chosen by God to, **"build My city" (Isa. 45:13).** This man had the heart that God was looking for so that His purposes could be fulfilled on the earth. We would do well to note what moves the hand and heart of God. Jerusalem needed to be rebuilt, and God chose Cyrus, a wealthy business king and in possession of all the resources he would need, to complete the task. He was not an Israelite, and yet God said of him, **"...He is my shepherd, and shall perform all my pleasure," (Isa. 44:28).**

What we need to see here are a number of very important keys that God used. He used a natural king—one who had wealth and one who cared about the things and purposes of God. Even though he was outside of the covenant, God wanted to example his heart. So God **anointed** him **(Isa. 45:1)** and this anointing allowed:

1. Nations to be subdued
2. The strength/armour of opposing kings to be loosed
3. Double Doors to open (double portion)
4. The gates that were opened would remain open to him

This all occurred so that God would ensure that the **"treasures of darkness"** and **"hidden riches of secret places"** may be discovered and given to Cyrus.

In the same way, God has anointed you as a business king. He has chosen you amongst many to be a marketplace success story, a financial provider for the projects of God on the earth. He has called you to amass wealth to help **"build His city"** on the earth. There is hidden treasure and secret riches that He wants you to discover and use. He has anointed you to do it. The one aspect in life that is closely guarded by the devil, particularly towards a Christian business king, is the free use of finance to see the spread of the gospel on the earth. God has ensured that you have what it takes to subdue the stronghold of this enemy. You are anointed to loose the armour of your opponents (so you can plunder their warehouses), be recipients of double portion provisions, and open the gates of the various, secretly hidden storehouses of wealth that the devil guards so stringently. The whole purpose of God wanting you to be a benefactor is because He has sworn an oath to "Israel" (His people) and He wants His influence freed to all the earth so that the captives can go free and people can find the Lord **(Isa. 45:13)**.

Apart from the actual monetary wealth that is laid aside for you, **Isa. 45:14** outlines that God has also purposed to give you:

1. The labour of Egypt
2. The merchandise of Cush
3. The stature of the Sabeans.

Where Israel was in ascendancy, they would enjoy the produce of Egypt, the wealth of Ethiopia and the stature of the Sabeans. However in the business world we need these three concepts working for us so we can be successful. Businesses do require a skilled **labour** force. Although this scripture is referring to the product that will become God's when the gospel has reached Egypt, God knows that in the marketplace you will need workers who are trained, able and willing to work hard with excellence. When there is a unity between owners and employees, the work output is of a high level. Boaz, in the book of Ruth, practiced a unique concept of **blessing** his workers in his greeting. He would say over them, **"The Lord be with you,"** and their response was, **"The Lord bless thee," (Ruth 2:4)**. When you blessed someone you were saying that God empowers them to succeed, have favour, prosper or add value to them and make them a benefit. Care and respect your labour force and desire God to be with them. Practice the release of blessing over their workstations and positions in the company.

Then God says He will open up the **merchandise** you will need to trade, and become successful with it. He will make sure you will have what you need so you can trade in the markets. As a final blessing, God will give you **stature** in your endeavours to capture the hearts of market-related people so that your business becomes sought after in the city.

This labour, merchandise, and stature will walk over to you, follow behind you, and be attached to you. God will do this! You will start to collide with wealth, that had previously been "hidden".

My Personal Motivation...

- God has appointed me. He has plans for allowing me to gain wealth.
- He has anointed me. His anointing in business will break open the fields that are set to provide for me.
- There are wealth and riches that remain hidden, but my purpose is to discover this secret supply and hidden treasure and it's the anointing He has allowed me to have that will procure it.
- I will trust Him to bring to me the labour, merchandise, and stature I will need, to be the King-in- business He has designed for me.

Nineteen

Supply and Opportunity

"But I rejoiced in the Lord greatly, that now at the last your care of me hath flourished again; wherein ye were also careful, but ye lacked opportunity."

(Philippians 4:10)

The hearts of God's financial kings have to mature in their calling and result in them becoming true, generous givers in the kingdom. Their abilities to give and sow are such that the kingdom can advance that much quicker. The classic example of business people being able to do things at a rapid pace is that of Ezra the faithful priest and Nehemiah, the business king. Ezra took approximately thirteen years to rebuild the temple, but Nehemiah took only fifty-two days to complete the walls around the city.

Business kings have an anointing to create wealth and to find solutions. They work quickly, making the decisions they need to make. They have to be able to see the opportunities that arise and have a witness that they are exactly that— opportunities. We don't like to look at things in this way but all through the Word, God motivates His business kings through the promise of returns, harvests, and supply. (see reference made to Pastor Mike Murdock p.56) He will provide them with ideas and opportunities to bring supply to their businesses. He wants them wealthy. He needs them to produce at healthy levels so that His kingdom can advance. God told the Israelites in **Malachi 3:8-10**, that tithing and giving offerings were one way to encourage returns and supply to your business or family. In fact He even said, " '...**prove me now herewith,' saith the Lord of hosts, 'if I will not open you the windows of heaven, and pour you out a blessing, that there shall not be room enough to receive it,'"** **(Mal. 3:10).** Elsewhere in **Luke 6:38**, God says, **"Give, and it shall be given unto you; good measure, pressed down, and shaken together, and running over, shall men give into your bosom. For with the same measure that ye mete withal it shall be measured to you again."** Looking through the Word I can a list a number ways where you see the promise of returns as a motivation from God. It's like God is saying, Take the step. Trust Me. See that I am good.

Paul comments in our scripture, that these Philippians had shown great care for him previously and even though they would have continued providing for him at the same level of care, they lacked the **opportunity** to do so. God arranges opportunity for you to give and bless. When these opportunities come, it will go well with financial kings to recognize what God is providing for them. God gives you opportunity to give so that He can create and arrange opportunities for you to receive supply in your business. A financial king's job is to create a flow of wealth into the kingdom. God is not opposed to him having large amount of money. He is anointed to succeed in the marketplace. One of the ways he is able to generate these kinds of supernatural returns is to see when an opportunity to give has arrived. As he responds, God opens up supply from heaven that keeps him current and growing consistently.

Jesus goes on to say, **"But my God shall supply all your need according to His riches in glory by Christ Jesus." (Phil. 4:19)** This verse is in direct relationship to those who see the bigger picture and sow freely into God's sent ministries. They understand the value of partnering with them and reap as a promise from God, **"and my God shall supply all your need..."** Business kings can have this guarantee. This is good economic sense. SOW INTO GOD'S ECONOMY.

My Personal Motivation...

- God wants to supply all His kings-in-business with the wealth they will need to complete their God-given tasks. God inspires me to enter into this realm with a promise of financial return. When I invest in money markets, unit trusts or companies that are renowned for successful investments, it's still all a risk. My returns depend on a number of factors that for the most part, I have no control over. But in the Word of God, I am guaranteed returns as a motivation from God. So the real question is, "Can I trust God more than the investment company?"

- I will look for opportunities to give generously. God says that a generous man will devise ways to be generous and through this spirit of generosity, he will stand **(Isa. 32:8)**. To know this truth would be very helpful when the world is in recession.

- Opportunity is a key in my cash flow success. I will look for these opportunities that God provides. I will pray for creative ways and ideas to come to me, above the norm. Whatever God created, He placed within it a seed to produce again. My business has seeds that perhaps I have not yet explored. I will look for the "seed within a seed" principle. What else can I do with what I have? What have I not seen that is an amazing opportunity for me?

Twenty

Unlocking Spoken Blessings

"But he whose descent is not counted from them received tithes of Abraham, and blessed him that had the promises."

(Hebrews 7:6)

Abraham returned to the "King's Valley" after his defeat of Chedorlaolmer in **Genesis 14**. This king had swept through the whole area, defeating everyone in his path. Then Abraham defeated him with 318 men. How was that possible? **Genesis 14:14** tells us that he chose these men from his own house. They were "sons" in the house. To have "sons-in-the-house" is the secret to success. You have a unity where God can command His blessing. There is very little a house cannot do when there is unity, faith, and belief that all things are possible. Churches that grow "financial sons," in my opinion, are moving in the right direction.

At that precise time, when Abraham was returning from the victory, Melchizedek arrived on the scene and is allowed to go onto "King's" turf. A business king would be very wise to allow his Priest or Set man onto his turf. They carry an anointing to bless and change boundary lines. As they pray, they increase your sphere of influence, and this is exactly what happened. Melchizedek operated as Priest and Prophet to Abraham **(v18-**

19). First, he broke bread with him and then he blessed him. Later he affirmed the prophetic word over him. He had communion with Abraham and in so doing he reminded Abraham who his resource was—it was God, with whom he had a covenant relationship. Then Melchizedek blessed him and spoke increase, favour, and success over him. Immediately Abraham responded by giving this Priest in his life a tenth of all the spoil of his battles. What a strategy for business kings!

Melchizedek received this tithe of the spoil that Abraham had amassed and **Hebrews 7:6** tells us that Melchizedek blessed him in return, who had the promises. To bless means to empower success-release-favour-prosper-benefit-add value. As soon as Abraham blessed his Priest by giving him a tithe of all spoils, Melchizedek responded in blessing Abraham, which resulted in the promises over his life becoming unlocked. It wasn't long after this that Abraham and Sarah were blessed with a son in their old age, which was a previous promise from God.

Every business king for God has promises that remain in line for him. As they honour and bless their man of God with a tithe of their spoil, it results in these promises being unlocked in their lives. The operation requires two significant keys:

1) Recognize who the man of God is in your life, and then sow a financial blessing to him from the profit of your business transactions. The man of God in your life is the one who shapes your destiny and purpose and who fathers the call of God over you.

2) The set man, or man of God in your life, must never receive your blessing without blessing you in return.

Abraham had tremendous promises hanging over his life. It was only as he gave to his man of God, who in time blessed him, that these promises were unlocked for him.

My Personal Motivation...

- I will see the reason why God has given me a Priest in my financial kingship. Make sure that I am positioned under a set man/woman of God that He has supplied for my business kingship. Ask questions like,
"Am I positioned correctly?"
"Do I have the right spiritual covering and balance?"
"Am I part of God's banner of Prophet-Priest-King synergy that HE has ordained for my good?"
- **Exod. 17:8-15** is the classic example of this banner that Joshua fought under. Joshua in this story is the king-in-the-marketplace and had to make headway in the financial markets. Moses, Aaron and Hur were on top of a mountain overlooking the battle, and as long as Aaron and Hur held up Moses's hands, Joshua prevailed in his purpose. Moses was the PROPHET. Aaron was the PRIEST and Hur was the BUSINESS KING. Under this banner, Joshua succeeded. **Verse 14** actually tells us that God wanted this victory written down as memorial for Israel to be recounted in Joshua's presence. God needed his business king to know exactly how the victory took place. Now we all know that God has a covenant name, "The Lord Our Banner," but this banner, Prophet-Priest-King, is an under banner over the function of financial kings. Under this synergy, God's kings will be successful in the marketplace.
- I will allow my Priest to operate the way God intended in my business, as he carries an anointing to loose the promises of God over my life.
- I will notice the synergy of Prophet-Priest-King and allow this synergy to create the winning strategy in my business. I will get connected where this is available, understood, and practiced.

CPSIA information can be obtained at www.ICGtesting.com
Printed in the USA
LVOW12s1628290514

387788LV00016B/887/P